S0-AQM-662

MOVERS, SHAKERS, & HISTORY MAKERS

DOROTHY VAUGHAN
NASA'S LEADING HUMAN COMPUTER

CONTENT CONSULTANT
JAMES SCHOMBERT, PhD
PROFESSOR OF PHYSICS
UNIVERSITY OF OREGON

BY DEIRDRE R.J. HEAD

CAPSTONE PRESS
a capstone imprint

Capstone Captivate is published by Capstone Press, an imprint of Capstone.
1710 Roe Crest Drive
North Mankato, Minnesota 56003
www.capstonepub.com

Library of Congress Cataloging-in-Publication Data
Names: Head, Deirdre, author.
Title: Dorothy Vaughan : NASA's leading human computer / by Deirdre R.J. Head.
Description: North Mankato, MN : Capstone Press, [2021] | Series: Movers, shakers, and history makers | Includes index. | Audience: Grades 4-6
Identifiers: LCCN 2020001049 (print) | LCCN 2020001050 (ebook) | ISBN 9781496684776 (hardcover) | ISBN 9781496688194 (paperback) | ISBN 9781496684974 (pdf)
Subjects: LCSH: Vaughan, Dorothy, 1910-2008—Juvenile literature. | United States. National Aeronautics and Space Administration—Biography—Juvenile literature. | African American women mathematicians—Biography—Juvenile literature. | Women mathematicians—Biography—Juvenile literature. | African American women—Juvenile literature.
Classification: LCC QA29.V32 H43 2021 (print) | LCC QA29.V32 (ebook) | DDC 510.92 [B]—dc23
LC record available at https://lccn.loc.gov/2020001049
LC ebook record available at https://lccn.loc.gov/2020001050

Image Credits
Alamy: Smith Collection/Gado Images, 30, The Picture Art Collection, 5; Library of Congress: Russell Lee/Farm Security Administration - Office of War Information Photograph Collection, 19, Warren K. Leffler/U.S. News & World Report Magazine Photograph Collection, 37; NASA: cover (foreground), 42, Bob Nye/LRC, 29, GRC, 26–27, Joel Kowsky/HQ, 39, LRC, 33, NACA Langley/LRC, 20–21, Sean Smith/LRC, 25; Red Line Editorial: 22; Shutterstock Images: Eric Glenn, 8, Everett Historical, 10–11, 13, 14, Jamie Lamor Thompson, 41, LeStudio, cover (background), 1, New Africa, 7

Editorial Credits
Editor: Charly Haley; Designer: Colleen McLaren

Printed in the United States of America.
PA117

CONTENTS

CHAPTER ONE
BEFORE REACHING THE STARS...........................4

CHAPTER TWO
LOOKING FOR WORK..................................12

CHAPTER THREE
USING MATH TO FLY...............................24

CHAPTER FOUR
BEING A HIDDEN FIGURE.......................36

TIMELINE...44
GLOSSARY..46
READ MORE/INTERNET SITES.............................47
INDEX...48

Words in **bold** are in the glossary.

BEFORE REACHING THE STARS

Young Dorothy Vaughan had no reason to imagine that people would someday send rockets into space. She was born in 1910 and the technology needed to explore space did not exist. There was no government program working to send humans into space and bring them back safely to Earth.

When Vaughan was a kid, she loved learning. She worked hard and became a great mathematician. Eventually she changed history by leading a team of people at the beginning of the U.S. space program.

Dorothy Vaughan studied a lot while growing up. She didn't know that one day she would use her knowledge to help people explore space.

5

As a black woman, Vaughan did not get a lot of credit for her work at the time. But decades later she was featured in the famous movie *Hidden Figures*. People everywhere learned about how she helped the United States start exploring space.

GROWING UP

Dorothy Vaughan was born in Kansas City, Missouri. As a child, her name was Dorothy Johnson. Dorothy's mother died when Dorothy was two years old. Dorothy's father, Leonard, then married Susie Peeler Johnson. Susie made sure Dorothy could read before she started school.

The Johnson family moved to West Virginia in 1917. Dorothy worked hard in school. She graduated from high school as **valedictorian**. She earned a full **scholarship** to go to college. She was only 15 years old at the time!

FACT

Dorothy's stepmother encouraged her to learn how to play piano. Later in life, Dorothy played piano for local churches to earn extra money for her family.

Dorothy was a quick learner. She learned to read at an early age.

The scholarship was to Wilberforce University in Ohio. Wilberforce was the state's oldest private historically black college. Although some historically black colleges have always allowed white students, they were established to educate black people. Dorothy studied math at Wilberforce. She did very well in her classes.

Howard and Wilberforce Universities are still educating students today.

After Vaughan graduated, her teachers told her to get a master's degree in math. She got a chance to attend Howard University, another historically black college. Vaughan was 19 years old. But ultimately she decided not to go to Howard.

HOWARD UNIVERSITY

If Vaughan had decided to go to Howard, she would have been part of the university's first master's degree program in math. A master's degree is a high-level college degree. Howard University was a very difficult college to get into. It is still difficult for students to get into Howard today. It is a famous and important university. Getting into the college was a huge accomplishment for Vaughan, even though she decided not to attend the school.

Many Americans were unable to work during the
Great Depression.

The Great Depression was happening in the
United States. The Depression was an **economic** crisis
that put many Americans out of work. Many families
like Vaughan's didn't have much money during this
time. Vaughan could help support her family if she

got a job instead of going to Howard. She could help
make sure that her sister had money for college.
Instead of going to Howard, Vaughan looked for a job
as a teacher.

CHAPTER TWO

LOOKING FOR WORK

It was 1929, and the United States needed more black teachers. The country was **segregated** at that time, especially in the south. This kept white and black people separated. White people and black people could not eat at the same restaurants or use the same water fountains. And the places for black people were always much worse than those for white people. Certain jobs were segregated. In the south, people were segregated in schools too. This meant that white teachers taught white students and black teachers taught black students.

Segregation meant black people could only go to certain places. These places were often labeled "colored," a historically offensive term that has since been replaced with terms of respect.

Teaching at black schools was one of the best jobs available to black women in the 1930s.

The enslavement of black people in the United States had ended in 1865. But the effects of it remained. Black people faced a lot of **discrimination**. Many white Americans did not see black people as their equals. That was one of the ideas left over from the era of slavery. Black Americans had fewer job opportunities available to them. Most of the jobs that black people could get did not pay as well as jobs for white people.

Women during this time didn't have many job choices either. Many people expected women to stay at home and care for their children.

THE DEPRESSION AND SCHOOLS

The Great Depression meant the government had less money to spend on schools. Schools for black students had already been getting less money than white schools. The schools were supposed to be equal. But schools for black children often had lower-quality buildings and supplies.

Single women who didn't have money
often worked as servants for wealthy families.
They also worked as nurses, dressmakers, or teachers.
Because Vaughan was a single black woman, it
seemed that being a teacher was one of the only jobs
she would be able to get.

STARTING HER CAREER

Schools that needed black teachers would call
black colleges. The colleges could then recommend
their graduates to fill open positions. This was how
Vaughan got her first job. She taught English and
math at a school in a small town in Illinois. But after
just one year, the school ran out of money and
shut down.

BLACK TEACHERS

Vaughan wasn't the only black teacher who needed to
find extra work. Virginia's white teachers were among the
lowest paid in the country, and the state's black teachers
were paid even less. Black teachers in Virginia made only
half as much money as white teachers.

Vaughan's next job was at a school in North Carolina. But soon that school ran out of money too. For a while, Vaughan worked as a waitress at a hotel in Virginia. In 1931, Vaughan got a job as a high school teacher in Farmville, Virginia. That's where she met Howard Vaughan.

Dorothy and Howard Vaughan got married. Soon they had four children. They didn't have a lot of money. But they worked hard to support their family. Howard Vaughan worked at hotels helping people with their bags. During the summer, he worked at fancy hotels in New York. In winter, he worked in Florida. He was away from home a lot for work.

Vaughan was always careful about how she spent money. She also took extra jobs when she could. One of these jobs was playing piano on Sunday mornings at a church. She kept looking for ways to support her family.

A RARE OPPORTUNITY

World War II (1939–1945) had begun, and the United States was now part of it. One day in 1943, Vaughan saw flyers at the post office advertising U.S. government jobs. She was interested in two of the jobs. One was a job doing laundry at a military base in Virginia. The other was a job for a female mathematician. Mathematicians were needed to help find ways to make better airplanes. Because the United States used airplanes for its military, the country wanted the best planes it could get.

WORKING WOMEN IN WORLD WAR II

During World War II, President Franklin D. Roosevelt opened more government jobs to women and people of color. That was because many white men were overseas fighting in the war. Women and black people could fill the open positions in the United States until the men returned from war. By 1945, the war had created jobs for more than 19 million women. The math job that Vaughan looked at was one of the new jobs that had opened for black women.

The United States wanted to build better airplanes to fight in World War II.

LMAL
33025

The U.S. government began hiring more women in 1941.

The math job was a rare opportunity for a black woman. The job would help defend the United States by working to make better military planes. Before 1941, women and black people could not have that type of job at all. White men had these

jobs, and they wouldn't hire women or black people. But in 1941, President Franklin D. Roosevelt banned discrimination in hiring for government jobs related to defending the country. After this, women and more people of color started getting hired for those jobs.

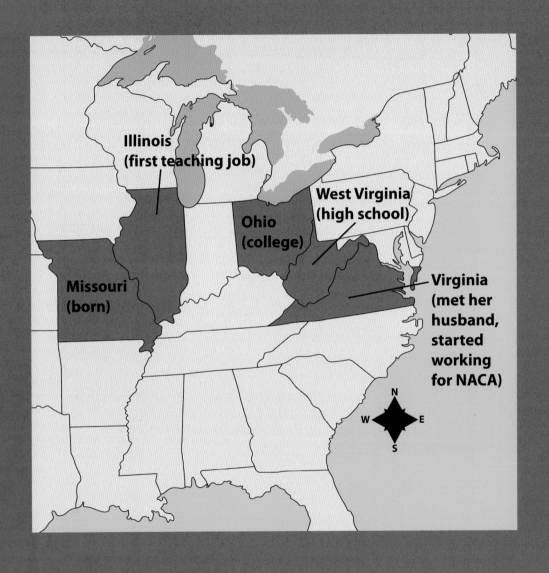

Illinois
(first teaching job)

Ohio
(college)

West Virginia
(high school)

Missouri
(born)

Virginia
(met her
husband,
started
working
for NACA)

But the southern United States was still segregated. It stayed that way until the 1960s. There were still not many job opportunities for black people.

Vaughan applied for both the laundry job and the math job. When she got an offer for the math job, she took it. The job was with the National Advisory Committee for Aeronautics (NACA). The work would challenge Vaughan's mind.

CHAPTER THREE

USING MATH TO FLY

Vaughan's job would be at NACA's Langley Memorial Aeronautical Laboratory in Hampton, Virginia. NACA was a government **agency** that researched flying technology. It did tests on how to make airplanes fly faster and for longer distances. NACA would eventually become the National Aeronautics and Space Administration (NASA). Mathematicians were an important part of this work.

Vaughan agreed to work at NACA for as long she was needed. NACA said her job there would not last longer than six months after World War II ended.

FACT

Vaughan didn't want to make a big deal out of getting her job at NACA. But the local black newspaper still included a sentence announcing her new job.

The Langley lab is still used by the U.S. government today.

NACA tested the Martin B–26 Marauder, a bomber plane, in 1943.

Vaughan began working at NACA in the fall of 1943. The lab was on a military base, and Vaughan had to move there for her job. Lab workers were required to live on the base.

Vaughan's job would keep her away from her friends and family for weeks and months at a time. She would be able to visit during her days off and on holidays. But the job paid her twice as much money as she made working as a teacher. This extra money would help her family a lot.

THE WEST COMPUTERS

The labs at Langley were segregated. On Vaughan's first day of work, she went to a room that was set up like a classroom. There, Vaughan learned she would be working as one of the West Computers. The West Computers was the name of a group of mathematicians. All of them were black women. Before electronic computers, computer was a job title for people. Computers used their math skills to solve difficult problems. They helped design vehicles that could fly into space.

Vaughan and the other West Computers had important jobs. But their workplace always reminded them that they were segregated. Their section of the Langley lunchroom was labeled with a cardboard sign.

FACT

At the time that Vaughan worked for NACA, the West Computers were the only black **professional** workers at Langley. Other black people worked as janitors and in the cafeteria.

NACA provided jobs to black women, including Mary Jackson of the West Computers, but the Langley lab was still segregated. Jackson continued to work for Langley until 1985.

Vaughan (left) with other NACA employees in 1950

The West Computers were not allowed to sit next to white workers. They could not even sit next to the white people who also worked as computers. The West Computers sat by the cardboard sign, but they tried to ignore it while they ate.

Despite the daily reminders of racism, the West Computers continued working. The group even took engineering classes. The women's hard work helped the United States make good fighting airplanes during World War II. As the West Computers' work grew, the U.S. government realized it would need these women to keep working after the end of World War II.

FIRST FEMALE SUPERVISOR

Vaughan became the West Computers' supervisor in 1949. She was the first black supervisor at NACA, and she was one of the few women to hold a supervisor's job. Being a supervisor meant that Vaughan was in charge of all the other West Computers. She had to understand everyone else's work, in case someone needed help.

Vaughan supervised the West Computers until 1958. That was the year that NACA became part of NASA. The West Computers division was then closed. Vaughan continued to work for NASA, though she was no longer a supervisor.

WORKING AT NASA

Vaughan worked for NASA for almost 30 years. Her work leading the West Computers helped start the United States' space program. She helped the program advance in flight and space technology.

THE FIRST TO SPACE

In the 1950s, the United States and the **Soviet Union** each sought to advance their space programs. The competition between these two countries was called the Space Race. The Soviet Union won the first major achievement in the Space Race when it launched the first satellite into space in 1957. Then in 1961, the Soviets put the first human astronaut into space. But the United States won the Space Race with its greatest achievement. American astronaut Neil Armstrong became the first human to walk on the moon in 1969.

A rocket launched by the Scout Launch Vehicle
Program in 1965

Vaughan worked on the Scout Launch Vehicle
Program. Scout was a group of rockets. It was used to
launch many satellites into space.

1957: The Soviet Union launches *Sputnik*, the first space satellite.

1961: The Soviet Union's Yuri Gagarin becomes the first man to orbit Earth.

1962: John Glenn becomes the first American astronaut to orbit Earth.

1963: The Soviet Union's Valentina Tereshkova orbits Earth 48 times.

1965: The United States sends a satellite to Mars.

1969: The United States' Neil Armstrong becomes the first human to walk on the moon.

In 1960 Vaughan began working with Langley's most advanced human computer group. The name of this group was the Analysis and Computation Division. Vaughan eventually became a computer engineer. This meant she had to change math into a formula that computers could understand.

Vaughan and her team were also responsible for the safety and success of astronaut John Glenn's space mission. He became the first American to orbit Earth in 1962.

CHAPTER FOUR

BEING A HIDDEN FIGURE

Throughout her career, Vaughan saw many significant changes in the United States. The civil rights movement fought against discrimination nationwide. Langley eventually stopped segregating its workers. Slowly, more opportunities opened up for black people as well as for women of all races. But it still took many years for the important work of Vaughan and the other West Computers to be recognized.

FACT

Members of Vaughan's team helped the United States with the Apollo 11 moon landing in 1969. Their work made it possible for astronaut Neil Armstrong to be the first human to set foot on the moon and return back to Earth safely.

A group marched in 1963 to protest against discrimination and segregation.

Vaughan was 61 years old when she retired from NASA in 1971. In the years after she retired, she was very involved with her church. She died on November 10, 2008, at age 98.

FACT

Katherine Goble Johnson worked with Vaughan at NACA. She said Vaughan was one of the smartest of all the West Computers. Johnson died in February 2020 at age 101.

Vaughan's life was remarkable. Unfortunately, few people knew about her accomplishments while she was alive. But Margot Lee Shetterly changed that. Shetterly grew up in Hampton, Virginia. When she was 18 years old, she visited her old church. She talked to her childhood Sunday schoolteacher, Kathaleen Land. Land happened be a retired mathematician from NASA. She had worked on the West Computers team at Langley. Land told Shetterly about the original human computers. She gave Shetterly the names of the women she remembered working with. One of these women was Vaughan.

Margot Lee Shetterly spoke at NASA in 2019 as part of a ceremony that honored the West Computers.

After that conversation, Shetterly wanted to learn more about the West Computers.

HIDDEN FIGURES

Shetterly's interest in the West Computers led her to write a book. It was called *Hidden Figures: The American Dream and the Untold Story of the Black Women Mathematicians Who Helped Win the Space Race.*

The book was released in September 2016. It became a best seller. Soon it was made into a movie called *Hidden Figures.* The movie starred actress Octavia Spencer as Vaughan. In December 2016, the movie opened in a few theaters. In January 2017, it was released to theaters across the country.

The movie was very popular. It was **nominated** for three Oscar awards. Vaughan and the other West Computers were now known for their part in history. Their work was not hidden anymore.

Octavia Spencer played Vaughan in the movie *Hidden Figures*.

Years after she worked for the U.S. space program, Vaughan's achievements became well known.

HIDDEN FIGURES WAY

In 2019, the *Hidden Figures* women were given another honor. After decades of having their work overlooked by the public, they had a road named after them. The road is called Hidden Figures Way. It is located in front of NASA's headquarters in Washington, D.C.

THE WEST COMPUTERS

THE FOUR WOMEN OF THE WEST COMPUTERS WHO RECEIVED CONGRESSIONAL GOLD MEDALS WERE:

- DOROTHY VAUGHAN
- CHRISTINE DARDEN
- KATHERINE GOBLE JOHNSON
- MARY JACKSON

Along with being recognized in the *Hidden Figures* book and movie, the group was given Congressional Gold Medals in 2019. The medals were to honor the West Computers' work with NASA. Vaughan was given her award **posthumously**.

Vaughan may have remained a "hidden figure" without Shetterly's book. Now Vaughan's story is well known. She helped the United States fly through the skies and into space. She also showed what hard work can help a person achieve.

TIMELINE

1910: Dorothy Vaughan (then Dorothy Johnson) is born in Kansas City, Missouri.

1929: After finishing college, Vaughan begins working as a teacher.

1932: Vaughan marries Howard Vaughan.

1943: Vaughan begins working for the National Advisory Committee for Aeronautics (NACA).

1949: Vaughan becomes the first black woman to work as a supervisor at NACA.

1958: NACA becomes the National Aeronautics and Space Administration (NASA).

1959: Vaughan works on NASA's Scout Launch Vehicle Program.

1969: NASA successfully sends people to the moon.

1971: Vaughan retires from NASA.

2008: Vaughan dies at the age of 98.

2016: Vaughan's life story is featured in a famous book and movie, both titled *Hidden Figures*.

GLOSSARY

agency (AY-juhn-see)
an office, often a part of government

discrimination (diss-krim-i-NAY-shuhn)
unfair behavior or unfair rules against people based on race, gender, age, or other traits

economic (ECK-o-nom-ick)
having to do with a country's money and resources

nominated (NOM-uh-nay-ted)
suggested to receive something, such as an award

posthumously (POHS-chuh-muhst-lee)
after the death of a person

professional (pruh-FESH-uh-nuhl)
related to a job that requires special training or schooling

scholarship (SKOL-ur-ship)
money that helps a person pay for college

segregated (SEG-ruh-gate-ed)
separated by race

Soviet Union (SOH-vee-et YOON-yuhn)
a former group of 15 republics that included Russia, Ukraine, and other nations in eastern Europe and northern Asia

valedictorian (vah-luh-dik-TOR-ee-uhn)
a student, usually with the highest grades, who gives a speech at the graduation ceremony

READ MORE

Feldman, Thea. *Katherine Johnson.* New York: Simon Spotlight, 2017.

Rissman, Rebecca. *Hidden Women: The African-American Mathematicians of NASA Who Helped Make America Win the Space Race.* North Mankato, MN: Capstone Press, 2018.

Wilkins, Ebony. *Katherine Johnson.* New York: DK Publishing, 2019.

INTERNET SITES

Hidden Figures **Official Website**
http://www.hiddenfigures.com

NASA: Dorothy Vaughan Biography
https://www.nasa.gov/content/dorothy-vaughan-biography

Women @ NASA
https://women.nasa.gov

airplanes, 18, 20, 24, 31
Armstrong, Neil, 32, 34, 36

churches, 6, 9, 17, 38

Great Depression, the, 10, 15

Hidden Figures, 6, 40–41, 42, 43
Howard University, 9, 11

Illinois, 16, 22

Johnson, Katherine Goble, 38, 43

math, 4, 7–9, 16, 18–20, 23, 24, 28, 35, 38–40
military, 18, 20, 26
Missouri, 6, 22

National Advisory Committee for Aeronautics (NACA), 22, 23, 24–26, 28, 31–32
National Aeronautics and Space Administration (NASA), 24, 32, 38, 42, 43
North Carolina, 17

rockets, 4, 33
Roosevelt, Franklin D., 18, 21

Scout Launch Vehicle Program, 33
segregation, 12, 23, 28, 36
Shetterly, Margot Lee, 38, 40, 43
Spencer, Octavia, 40

teachers, 9, 11, 12, 16–17, 22, 27, 38

Virginia, 16, 17–18, 22, 24, 38

West Computers, 28, 30–32 36–41, 43
West Virginia, 6, 22
Wilberforce University, 7, 9
World War II, 18, 24, 31